AF251364

Fashion Beyond Borders

Exploring the Global Fashion Industry

First Edition

SHAWNIE GRANT

ISBN: 978-0-692-17954-3
Shawnie Grant- Houston, Texas

ACKNOWLEDGMENTS

On behalf of its author, Fashion Beyond Borders: Exploring The Global Fashion Industry expresses its sincere appreciation to Bertram Grant Sr., James Grant Jr., JoAnn Woodard, and Titra L. Whitted, who contributed their ideas and suggestions to create this first edition. We are grateful for New York University Shanghai High School Academy for creating the opportunity for Fashion Beyond Borders: Exploring the Global Fashion Industry fashion course to be taught at their university to students during the summer program. We are also grateful for Texas Southern University, where this book is sold in the Barnes and Nobles college bookstore. Thank you to High Fashion Homes for allowing us to use your store to create material to promote and market this book.

To The Reader

May this knowledge open a new world for you,
and place you in harmony with your passion.

This is my intention for you and for all.

CONTENTS

PREFACE

In this fashion course book you will find fashion gems creatively designed by the author, which provide you with invaluable insight into what to do and what not to do while producing a fashion brand. This book also provides step-by-step guides to help you learn how to manufacture a fashion brand, as well as learn about a variety of career choices within the fashion industry. It's a how-to book in the broadest sense of term. This book will test your critical thinking skills with questions that present you real life scenarios in which you may encounter obstacles while in the process of manufacturing your fashion brand. This book features:

- Complete instructions for creating a fashion portfolio to present when applying to fashion schools and fashion companies, or to simply use as a guide to start a fashion brand.
- A formula to successfully manufacture a fashion brand on a large or small scale.
- The perfect strategies to market and sell your fashion products to consumers and businesses.
- Descriptions of multiple fashion jobs with hopes to guide you into the exact position that excites you so that you may discover your passion and talents.
- A glossary with business and fashion terminology.
- Critical thinking questions that will immerse you into a variety of real life situations when manufacturing a fashion brand in China.

This book was inspired by Shawnie Grant's experience creating and teaching the six day fashion curriculum Fashion Beyond Borders: Exploring the Global Fashion Industry at New York University Shanghai for the NYUSPS annual summer program. It also includes her personal journey by sharing the obstacles that she experienced while living in China for two years in order to project manage the production of her clothing brand, and the decisions she made to overcome them.

All who read, understand, and apply this knowledge will be better prepared to manufacture and launch a fashion brand, as well as start the process of entering into a career within the fashion industry.

Ni Hao! Greetings in Chinese.

A Preview

Guess what this drawing is used for:
a. Product advertisement
b. Seam measurements
c. A fashion portfolio

Most likely the job title for the person that created this drawing is:
a. A fashion buyer
b. An image consultant
c. A fashion designer

The target audience for this fashion design is:
a. Fashion forward women
b. Female college students
c. Plus size women

1

DISCOVERING YOUR PASSION

"Those who dare to be creative are free from limitations."

Shawnie Grant
Author

Discovering your talents and area of interest in fashion can be an exciting yet overwhelming journey. With a variety of sectors to choose from, identifying your abilities may sometimes require you to work in several positions within the industry. Your attitude will determine if you will feel frustrated or have fun while wearing multiple hats to discover exactly what it is about fashion that you are passionate about. The first question to ask is: what gets me excited about fashion? Some people enjoy **designing** clothes by **sketching** their ideas on drawing pads, while others enjoy matching and pairing clothes with accessories to create different looks. It didn't take me long to realize that I didn't enjoy sewing clothes but I do enjoy sketching ideas for clothes. I highly suggest getting involved in a few fashion projects in your city in order to learn the job duties required for different positions. The second question to ask yourself is: where do I usually draw inspiration from? Knowing the answer to this question can play a strong role in guiding you to define the area of fashion you are passionate about.

Stay aware of what's going on around you. **Inspirations** present themselves every day in different forms. Many fashion designers have mentioned that some of their inspirations for **color combinations** and scenes for photo shoots have been discovered while they were walking down the street. Inspiration can come from noticing cool **photo props** along the road, or while walking in nature and seeing a beautiful, colorful bird, which may spark ideas for color combinations for a spring collection. Inspiration can also be found in museums, movies, music videos, or from creative works from designers in the past. Once you learn what it is that excites you within the fashion industry, it will lead you to the career that you are most interested in, which may end up being your passion. For example, if you love receiving fashion inspiration from characters on TV shows and sharing those **fashion tips** online with your family and friends, perhaps your passion is working as a **fashion blogger**. I thought that I wanted to own and manage a boutique selling custom-made clothes to men and women, but within six months, I realized that I wanted to focus on being creative by designing and manufacturing clothes. The exciting part about having a career within the fashion industry is that there aren't any limits. You can work in several positions and be as creative as you desire. Explore fashion beyond borders.

2

INTRODUCTION TO FASHION DESIGN

Fashion design is the art of designing clothes and accessories. Because fashion design is influenced in a number of ways, a designer must always consider changes in **consumer** taste. In order to keep up with new styling trends, designers must research trending items and interpret them to their **target audience.**

Learning **fashion seasons** is essential when choosing colors, fabrics, and release dates for your clothing brand. Before you get started on a fashion portfolio, think about which fashion season you would like to create your first collection for. Fashion is split into four seasons: Spring/Summer, Fall/Winter, Resort, and Pre-Fall. The two major seasons, however, are Spring/Summer and Fall/Winter. Spring/Summer starts in January and ends around June, and Fall/Winter is from July to December. Resort collections overlap the first two seasons and are offered from late October through December. Pre-Fall collections are placed in stores a bit before Fall/Winter collections come in.

It's pretty easy to see why these seasons cause much confusion. In January it's still very cold, so you may wonder why Spring/Summer and Resort collections would be for sale in stores around the globe. The reason is because fashion's retail calendar is different from the traditional calendar. Retailers like to start selling spring clothes early before the actual season begins. Fall merchandise arrives in stores around July, to make a profit from back-to-school shoppers. When a new season comes in, you'll notice the prior season will generally go on sale or clearance. All of these strategies are used to maximize sales.

Before you get started with your fashion portfolio, think about which season you would like to create a collection for. Some designers choose to focus on one season, while others choose to design collections for all seasons. There are fashion brands that offer all year around collections, meaning that you can transition the garments from Spring/Summer to Fall/Winter with a change of accessories, tops, or bottoms. For example, adding a pair of winter leggings to wear under a pair of shorts and matching it with cute ankle boots and a sweater, transitions summer attire to create a Fall/Winter look. In the illustration below, the white button down blouse would be considered an all year around garment, which means you could find it on the clothing racks during the Spring/Summer and Fall/Winter season. This fashion illustration was created using a fashion design software by a professional fashion illustrator living in India.

Choosing Fabrics For Your Designs

When the moment comes to choose fabrics, the Fall/Winter season usually presents a wide range of garments produced with **leather, wool, suede, velvet, twill, and heavy cottons** made in darker colors, while the Spring/Summer season usually present **collections** in light fabrics such as **silk, chiffon**, and **cotton** produced in bright, vibrant colors.

Textiles such as **lace** and **sheer** are commonly used to design wedding dresses, while **taffeta** is used to produce **fashion-forward formal attire**. **Denim** and fabric with prints are usually used to produce casual, fashionable **attire**. **Polyester** is commonly used to produce active wear and swimsuits due to its stretch and comfort. This fabric is also blended with other fabrics when used to create **ready-to-wear** garments that stretch to fit a woman's curves.

Once a fashion designer has decided which season they would like to design for, confirmed their designs and the type of fabrics that they would like to use for their collection, the next step is creating a **fabric story** for the collection. In most cases, fashion designers will have different fabric stories for each collection in order to differentiate the collections that share the same season. Most designers will also decide their fabric story before purchasing fabrics for their designs. For example, some fashion designers will use the same flower print fabric to produce all of their fashion designs for their new collection. Therefore, flowers are a part of the fabric story. A fabric story can also be created with colors instead of print patterns. Knowing who your target audience is will assist you with choosing your fabric story. American women 60 years and up most likely won't wear a collection of garments that has a fabric story with the colors hot pink mixed with purple, and most curvy women prefer to wear stretch fabrics. Therefore, your target audience, designs, fabrics, and color choices are all important factors when creating a clothing brand.

The process of materializing a design will require the designers to submit their **specs** to **manufacturers**. This is the essence of a fashion designer's role; however, there is variation within this that is determined by **merchandising** and budgeting needs. For example, budget **retailers** will use inexpensive fabrics to create trendy garments, but high-end retailers will ensure that quality fabrics are used to offer garments that can be worn for several seasons in the future.

Starting a career as a fashion designer will require sketching out your ideas. If you aren't confident with your drawing skills, don't worry. You may be surprised to learn that there are many fashion designers that don't know how to sketch. When this is the case, a fashion designer will have to hire another designer or an artist to sketch the designs. A fashion designer can also hire a **fashion illustrator** to make their ideas come to life by creating digital **fashion illustrations**.

Fashion Gems

I highly recommend fashion designers to join an art or fashion design class to learn the basics of sketching and shading techniques to save time and money in the long run. This avoids the hassle of having to hire a second party to work for you. You have to wait for their availability to start your project, negotiate a completion time of your order, as well as pay the fees for their services rendered. Instead, try to do your own sketching. You can purchase a sketchbook that has **fashion croquis** to make it easier for you to create your fashion designs on your own. If you are more tech savvy, consider investing in a fashion design software that allows you to learn how to create digital fashion designs. Designing your clothes with fashion design software may lessen the skills needed for drawing and sketching which allows you to have more time to imagine and design. There are a variety of sketch books and fashion design software available online and in bookstores.

Now that you have started thinking about your target audience, fashion seasons, fabrics, and how to put your fashion ideas on paper, it's time to get your creative juices flowing and create your fashion portfolio.

3

CREATING A FASHION PORTFOLIO

A fashion portfolio is a representation of you and should show off your skills and specialization. For example, skills such as draping, pattern making, drawing, water painting, etc. Specializations such as children's clothes, women's clothes, swimwear, etc. Your portfolio should consists of: a mood board, the **process**, technical flats, drawings of the final looks, fabric swatches, a cover, and an end page. Your portfolio can also include physical artifacts such as flowers, pictures, fabric, or other materials. A portfolio can also consist of different **series** to showcase more than one collection but each series should have it's own mood board, process, technical flats, drawings, and fabric swatches. Keep in mind that when adding more than one series to your portfolio, the overall theme of the portfolio should remain the same. For example, is your theme about plants and nature or are all of your collections created from organic materials? It's typical for a portfolio to consist of 4-6 series. Your strongest series should be placed first inside of the portfolio to capture the viewer's attention. Your second strongest series should be the last series in the portfolio. A person viewing your portfolio should be able to understand it without you being there to explain it. Making sure that your vision is clear before creating a fashion portfolio is essential. I highly recommend that you start the creative process with a vision board.

A vision board is a great start to create the theme for your fashion portfolio. Some designers create **vision boards** before creating their fashion portfolio; however, this step isn't required. A vision board plays an important role when trying to convey your ideas to your design team and anyone involved in the creation of your **fashion portfolio.** A vision board usually consists of visual ideas that align with the ideas that you have for how you want to create your fashion portfolio. It lessens the percentage of your team being confused about the direction you are going for your clothing brand. For example, if you desire to create a fashionable, quality swimsuit brand, you might add images of Victoria's Secret swim suit line to your vision board, along with images of colors or anything that will deliver the overall idea to your design team.

Even when working alone on a fashion project, I prefer to create a vision board to help me stay focused on the theme of my clothing collection before creating my fashion portfolio. When choosing from a variety of inspirations to assist with the creative process of your clothing brand, one can easily become distracted and get off track when putting the overall look together. Starting off with a vision board requires a little more effort, but it is worth it because it can decrease the percentage of errors, which in the end saves you money.

Before I realized the significance of a vision board, I created a fashion portfolio that consisted of different fashion designs that didn't complement each other after being assembled into a single collection. My **theme** was all over the place because I didn't have a solid vision before starting the designing process of the clothing brand. This may not seem like a big deal, but when you have deadlines to meet and are faced with an error, you may have to postpone the release date of your clothing brand in order to correct the problem. If you are a designer employed by a fashion company, this can cause the sales and marketing team to miss deadlines for their goals.

Fashion designers with experience may choose to omit creating a vision board and choose to start with creating a **mood board** for their fashion portfolio. Mood boards are very similar to vision boards and in some cases a vision board is referred to as a mood board. When creating a mood board for a fashion portfolio, the layout will be different. The mood board will consist of your own fashion designs instead of images from a magazine. A mood board for a fashion portfolio is structured to create a professional look, while a vision board will consist of a free flow of images and words. Below is a fashion illustration of a vision board for a glam studio. Notice that the images are freely placed all over the board and not structured in a formal layout. This fashion illustration was created using a fashion design software by a professional graphics designer living in India.

Professional designers and fashion design students usually create a **fashion collage,** which is similar to a vision board except all of the images used for the board are usually clothes, accessories, or fashion related items. There are many art and design processes that you can use to put your ideas on paper before making your ideas come to life on the runway. Choose the option best for you.

Now that we know the differences between and benefits of a fashion collage, vision board and mood board, let's go through the step-by-step process of creating them.

How to Make a Vision Board

Step 1: Decide your target audience, theme, and fashion season for your clothing brand. Look up your favorite fashion designers and watch some of their past fashion shows to get an idea on how you can get creative with themes. Try to guess their target audience by observing the models, hairstyles, colors, and accessories. It's helpful to view more than one fashion designer.

Step 2: Choose inspirational images, colors, and text that you will use for your vision board to deliver the theme of your clothing brand. You can find images for your vision board in magazines or online. "Fashion forward," "active wear," or "vintage" are examples of words that can be added to a vision board to describe the kind of clothing brand you're aiming for.

Step 3: Create your vision board by taping or gluing the images and text on a poster board. Inspirations may include hairstyles, cars, art, accessories, or anything that inspired the theme of your collection. A vision board will display the lifestyle of the type of brand you will create. If you are tech savvy, you can create a digital vision board to save money and help the environment. Simply find images online and insert them into a PowerPoint presentation or slideshow on your computer. Once your vision board is complete, share it with your team. Or, if you are working alone, use it as the template to start the process of creating your fashion portfolio.

How to Make a Mood Board

If you have a design team, work closely with them to create a mood board. A mood board is a description of your fashion collection. It's a written description and collection of images to give viewers an idea of how your fashion brand will look in your portfolio. A mood board is the first page and is used as an introduction to the rest of the collection in the portfolio.

Step 1: Create a **written description**. This description is usually brief, consisting of about 3-4 sentences. Add information about your target audience, theme, and season. It's also important that all models, sketches, technical drawings, or illustrations in the portfolio are aligned with your target audience.

Example 1: If your description mentions that your target audience is young girls, your models/illustrations should look like young girls, not women.

Example 2: If the theme for your clothing brand is Spring/Summer 70's fashion, the designs in your portfolio may consist of high waist, bright, vibrant- colored, fitted pants that have flare legs.

Step 2: Create a **fashion drawing**. Your drawing should be complete with color and be included on the same page as the written description. Only one drawing is needed for the mood board, but a designer has the freedom to add as many models as he/she chooses to set the mood for the collection. Keep in mind that the mood board is usually one page, but as a designer you have the freedom to add innovation.

Step 3: Complete your mood board by adding a sample piece of fabric to the page. The sample fabric is used to show viewers the exact fabric that will be used to manufacture the clothes. Add sample fabric by cutting a small square shaped piece of fabric from the fabric roll of your choice, apply glue to the back side of the fabric, and stick it on the top or bottom of the page, preferably in the corner. You may also use a colored pencil or marker to show viewers the colors that will be used for the fabric. Designers usually use this option when they don't have fabric available to add to the portfolio. Simply use the same colored pencils that were used for your fashion illustration, draw a small box, and fill it with the color. The amount of colors that you are using for your designs will determine the amount of colored boxes that you will need to add to each fashion drawing. Some designers will choose to use a design software which allows them to have their digital fashion designs and fabrics printed by a printing company. Below is an illustration of a mood board. Remember to elaborate in your written description. The mood board sets the tone for the entire portfolio. This mood board was created using a fashion design software by a professional fashion illustrator living in India.

Theme

Country western

Description

Cowboy hats and boots.
Decorated men jackets
and shirts.

Style

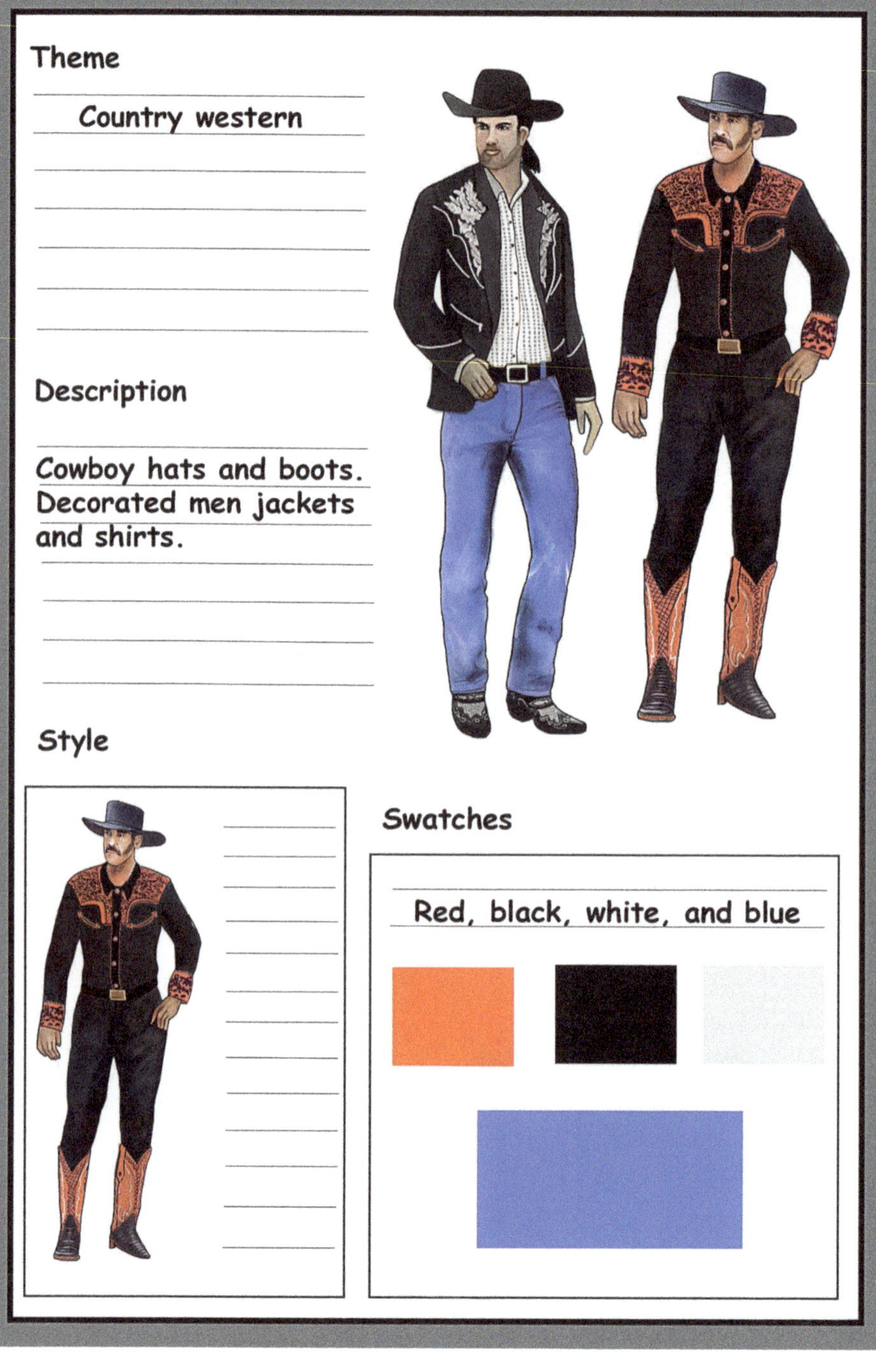

Swatches

Red, black, white, and blue

Fashion Gems
Sketching, Shading, and Color Techniques: Choose a croquis that you like, as this will make sketching your vision easier. You should start your drawing with a pencil so you can erase errors. You don't have to draw a face or hair, but some designers will do it to deliver the full look of how the model can be styled. Once you are happy with your sketch, you can trace your design with ink. Next, shade the design with colored pencils, which can be fun and give a beautiful look to any drawing. Sharpen your colored pencils to a fine point and start coloring the garments with light pressure. Once the entire garment has color, color over the areas that you want darker 2-3 more times. The more layers of color you add, the darker the garment will become. Pressure shading can also be used, but it's usually done by designers with a little more experience. These techniques will give you a smooth, professional fashion drawing. I highly recommend that you take an art class or purchase a how-to book on sketching to learn more about sketching, coloring, and shading techniques. Below are digital fashion illustrations created with a fashion design software. A fashion illustrator using a design software will have to sketch the fashion design before transferring it to the computer to create a digital illustration. When using digital illustrations for a fashion portfolio, the designer will have the portfolio professionally printed and formatted into a book.

Making Your Fashion Design Pages

Now that your mood board is completed, it's time to create your fashion designs and **technical drawings**—also known as **flat drawings**—for your portfolio. Create a technical drawing for each fashion design. Technical drawings are very important when you are ready to produce your clothing brand. They provide the **seamstress** and **tailors** with detailed information about **seam measurements** and placement of buttons, zippers, and other **embellishments** to the **garment**. If you don't provide technical drawings to a factory, this can increase the chance that your clothes will not fit your customers the way you imagined. Technical drawings should include seam measurements for each section of the garment and all details for the garment when submitting **specs** to a manufacturer. Below are digital illustrations of basic flat drawings without seam measurements and specific details for the garments. If the illustration below was presented to a manufacturer, they would immediately request seam measurements for each clothing size that you plan to offer along with instructions for the type of fabric to use, and placements of zippers and buttons. This illustration was created using a design software by a fashion design student living in Shanghai, China.

Fashion Gems

The first time that I had a manufacturer create clothing samples for me, I provided them clothing samples to copy without submitting a specs sheet because I decided to use the factory's measurement chart to create a variety of sizes. Long story short, it didn't take me long to realize that everyone's measurement chart is different even if they have the same target audience as you. The best way to ensure that your clothing brand will fit your target audience the way you want is by choosing your own models so that you create your own measurement chart. Below is an illustration of men and women body shapes. Choose the body shapes that you are designing clothes for, arrange a fitting with models that match the body shape, and take their body measurements with measuring tape to create a measurement chart for all of the sizes that you will offer. The illustration below was created using a design software by a fashion design student living in India.

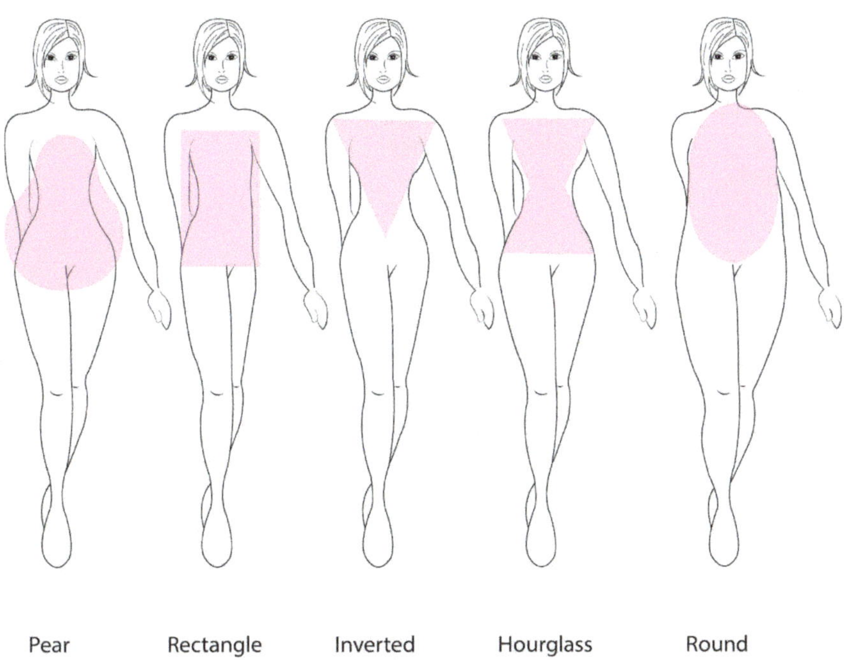

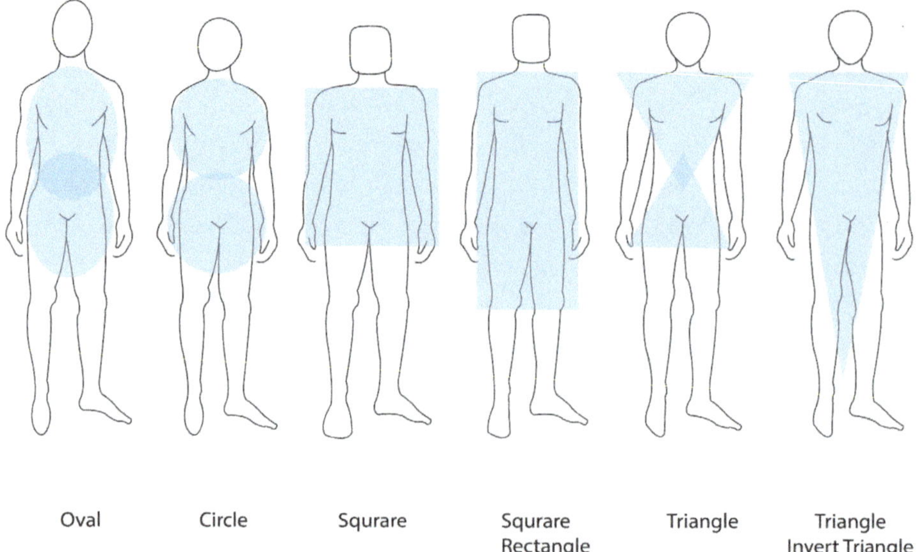

In your fashion portfolio, each page of a design collection should include:

1. the fashion design
2. the technical drawing for the fashion design
3. the pieces of sample fabric that will be used to manufacture the design

For example, if you are creating a Fall/Winter collection consisting of 12 designs, you will need 12 pages of paper. There needs to be one fashion design along with a technical drawing on each page. You can divide the fashion designs between you and your design team if you are working with others. All ideas for the fashion designs should be discussed and approved by your entire team before you start creating the fashion designs or technical drawings. It's very important that you consult with your entire team throughout the process to ensure that everyone is working in harmony and staying focused on the overall theme of your clothing brand. Below is a scanned copy of a drawing created by a beginner level fashion design student. The drawing was used in a fashion portfolio. The technical drawing below is fine for your fashion portfolio but seam measurements and specs need to be added when submitting the design to the clothing manufacturer.

Assembling Your Fashion Portfolio

The last step before binding your portfolio is to create a cover and an end page. A cover should list you and your team of designer's names, and should also include one visual. This visual should be an image that describes your entire fashion portfolio. In the same way the cover of a music album describes the music within, the image on the cover of your fashion portfolio should represent the emotion of your fashion designs. The end page provides answers to the cover and rounds up the story of the portfolio.

Now that you have completed the cover page, end page, the mood board, fashion designs, technical drawings, and added fabric samples, it's time to categorize your designs and compile all of the pages.

The order of the pages should be as follows:

1. cover page
2. mood board
3. fashion designs with technical drawings and fabric samples on each page
4. end page

Fashion Gem

If you have a collection that includes designs of dresses and pants, you can put the dresses together and the pants together. You can be as creative as you like when coming up with ideas to create and assemble your fashion portfolio but remember to keep it professional if you plan to present it to a fashion company or fashion school.

To bind your portfolio, there are several options available. You can place the fashion pages inside page protectors with holes and bind the pages together with metal rings, or add the pages into a binder folder. More experienced fashion designers will use portfolio books of higher quality, have all of their work professionally printed into a portfolio book, or make an accordion with the pages. Alternatively, tech savvy designers may choose to create digital fashion portfolios. Creating a digital portfolio with fashion illustrations will require the proper software.

Congratulations! You have successfully created a fashion portfolio. Fashion portfolios are key to applying for jobs at large fashion firms or fashion schools. It's a visual resume of your experience and is sometimes a requirement to be hired for a job or for school admission. There are several different ways that you can design the layout of your fashion portfolio; therefore, don't limit yourself—get creative!

If you are confident in your designs and want to proceed with starting a clothing brand, the next step is manufacturing.

4

MANUFACTURING A CLOTHING BRAND

Step 1: Sourcing Materials

Materials to produce and package clothes can include—but are not limited to—the following: **clothing labels**, **care instructions**, **hang tags**, fabric, zippers, buttons, and any material that is used to create the clothes.

Finding a reliable supplier for your fabric and materials is essential to achieving high quality garment production. But keep in mind that you should keep your **production costs** low. Save yourself time and money by sourcing almost all of the necessary fabrics and materials within your country. Sourcing materials outside of your home country will only benefit you if you are purchasing bulk, wholesale orders. Sometimes you can find small vendors or factories overseas that will sell small quantities of supplies for a decent price. When sourcing fabric and materials from outside of your home country, the **MOQ** can be quite high, **import charges** and duties can be prohibitive, and the time frame to transport your materials from the factory to the destination can cause the production process to take longer.

Establish relationships with suppliers in order to negotiate the production cost and the MOQ. Some large manufacturers will accept smaller clothing orders if they believe that you will be a valuable customer in the future. Your job is to convince the manufacturer that you will order larger quantities on a regular basis in the future in order to receive a production price that you are comfortable with.

Fashion Gems

It will be most beneficial to produce with a manufacturer that will provide the service to source the materials and fabric needed to create your fashion brand. Many clothing manufacturers already have established relationships with fabric factories, and some clothing manufacturers have their own inventory of fabric for you to choose from. Therefore, the process of sourcing materials and fabric can become easier if you decide to let the clothing manufacturer source the materials for you. This method allows you to still have control of choosing the fabrics and material that you desire and relieves you of having to source a fabric factory and a clothing manufacturer all at once. To do this, simply inform the clothing manufacturer of the type of fabric that you want, and they will start the search. Some designers may suggest that you purchase your own materials and fabric to avoid paying a higher price due to the markup that the clothing manufacturer will add for sourcing the materials. However, you must be mindful that a fabric factory will also have a MOQ. Therefore, if you only want to have a total of 30 garments produced in taffeta and silk fabric, and the fabric factory MOQ is 300 meters per fabric, you will experience some frustration while trying to search for a fabric factory that offers quality materials with a MOQ that's within your budget. If you are producing your fashion brand outside of your city, state, or country, ask the manufacturer to mail you some **fabric swatches** so that you can touch and feel the quality before submitting an order. Be sure to double check if the fabric is in stock or not before submitting orders for your clothing production. Once, I purchased fabric online from a textile factory and was notified later that the fabric was out of stock. This may not seem like a big deal but when you have deadlines to meet, this situation can cost you a successful sale. If a fashion buyer has ordered and purchased a particular fabric for their wholesale order that is no longer available, you will be faced with having to repeat the process of presenting fabrics to your buyers to correct their order. This will make you appear as an amateur and can have an end result of you not being contacted for future purchases.

Step 2: Finding a Clothing Manufacturer

Finding a clothing manufacturer can be more difficult than you think. There are thousands of manufacturers to choose from. Trying to produce with manufacturers outside of your country can be expensive if you are a small business with a small production order. It's common to try out a few manufacturers until you find one that best fits your needs. The best way to source a manufacturer for fabric and clothing production is by performing an online search for clothing manufacturers in the city, state, or country that you desire to produce in. Once you find a few interesting factories, have your clothing samples produced with more than one manufacturer so that you can compare the quality and learn which manufacturer will best fit your needs. Sourcing more than one clothing manufacturer is very important if you have more than one clothing collection that requires different **sewing techniques** and sewing machines.

Once you have your clothing samples, test the quality by wearing and washing the samples. This will allow you to know the quality of the fabric and construction of the clothes before ordering in bulk. For example: if you wash a clothing sample and the color of the fabric lightens or if it shrinks, you have a few options:

A) Purchase a different brand of fabric
B) Be sure to mention on the care labels how-to care for the garment (cold wash, hand wash, or dry clean only to prevent shrinkage or fading of colors)

The key things to look for when sourcing a manufacturer are:

A) **Type of Manufacturer:** One may think that any clothing factory can produce any category of clothes. But the fact is, each clothing manufacturer specializes in different types of clothes. Example: if you're starting a fashion brand of winter coats, it would be wise to search for coat manufacturers. The seamstress and tailors will be experts at cutting and sewing patterns and materials for coats. There are clothing factories that produce more than one type of garment, but using a factory that solely focuses on winter coats will increase your chances of getting the quality garment that you hoped for. Different garments require specific sewing machines; therefore, a sewing machine used to produce blue jeans will be different from a sewing machine used to produce a t-shirt.

B) **MOQ:** If you plan to start small and produce 50 **units** per design, there is no need to contact a manufacturer that has a MOQ of 1,000 units per design. Most likely they won't negotiate a MOQ that is 950 units less than the amount they are requesting. A manufacturer that has a MOQ of 100 units per design will most likely negotiate with you if you convince them that you will be a valuable customer. The key is to find a factory that has a MOQ that's affordable for you. Keep in mind, the smaller the order, the more expensive your order will be per unit. Regardless of this, I highly recommend that you start small if you are a new business or entrepreneur selling online. The last thing you want is a large inventory of clothes sitting around that won't sell.

C) **Lead Time:** This is the time frame when you and the manufacturer will consult about the designs, seam measurements, materials, production cost, and all detailed information that involves the start to finish process of your fashion brand. The time frame of this process can vary depending on how punctual you and the factory are with responding to questions and concerns.

D) **Production Time:** This is the time frame that is needed to produce your fashion brand. Depending on the size of your order, the amount of staff working at the manufacturer, and the amount of other clothing orders that were submitted before your order, the amount of time needed can vary anywhere from 2 to 6 weeks for a clothing factory located in China. If you are producing within the country that you reside and there is a limited number of manufacturers, the time frame to produce your brand can even take months. This information should be discussed and confirmed between you and the manufacturer during the lead-time process before producing the order.

E) **Shipping Time:** This is the time frame that is needed to transport your fashion brand by air or sea delivery. Depending on the shipping carrier, shipping your parcel by air can arrive at your doorstep within 3-5 days. When shipping by sea, your **shipping container** can take 25-35 days to arrive at the port nearest to you. This information is very important when choosing a manufacturer to produce your clothes. Many manufacturers use the same shipping carriers but there are some manufacturers that will use different shipping carriers and have limited options to choose from. If you have a goal to produce a brand within 3 months and the shipping carriers that are contracted with the manufacturer will take up to 25-30 days, you may want to consider using a different manufacturer if they don't have better options. This will allow you to set aside more time for the production of your fashion brand in case there are any defects detected in the clothing during the quality control process. This method also allows you to have more time in case your order gets held up at customs for any reason.

F) **Production Capacity:** This information informs you of the amount of clothes that are being produced per month or year by the manufacturer. This will let you know if the manufacturer has the manpower required to produce your brand before your deadline.

G) **Price Point:** Once you have submitted your specs to the manufacturer, confirmed your fabric and all other requested information by the factory, the manufacturer will give you quotes for each design. Each design requires the seamstress or tailors to create patterns, and requires different sewing techniques. Therefore, each design will have a different price. For example: if your fashion brand is women's skirts and one skirt is short with pleats and the second skirt is a pencil skirt, the short, pleated skirt will most likely cost more since it requires more work to create pleats. If you are producing your fashion brand in Asia, your production price can be negotiated if the manufacturer is convinced that you will be a valuable customer in the future. Please keep in mind that if you negotiate the production price too low, this can result in the manufacturer cutting costs by producing your fashion brand with cheaper materials, which in the end can result in you having a lower quality brand.

H) ODM/OEM: An original equipment manufacturer, or OEM, simply means that a manufacturer produces their own fashion designs and allows retail companies and buyers to purchase the factory's ready-made collection and put their company's brand name on the clothing labels. If you decide to purchase **ready-made clothes** from a manufacturer, add your labels to it, and sell it, ODM/OEM is something you should inquire about when sourcing a clothing manufacturer. Most boutiques, fashion wholesalers, and online retail stores like to purchase ready-made clothes and add their brand name to it by changing the clothing labels. This is usually done when a buyer doesn't want to design clothes but sell trendy clothes.

Step 3: Creating Your Patterns
In order to create a **pattern** for your clothes, first you need to create **technical drawings**. The reason why you should start with technical drawings is that the manufacturers need them to know the specifications of your design in order to make it as instructed and provide you with production cost. They can't calculate production cost from looking at a fashion drawing or illustration without detailed information such as seam measurements and the amount of material to use. Patterns are extremely important because they will increase the percentage of your clothing samples turning out the way you desire if they are crafted correctly. A designer should always approve patterns with the factory before any fabric or material is used to produce clothing samples. Patterns are usually made with paper and clothing samples can be made using **muslin.** This method is highly suggested because it allows you to save money while correcting mistakes on your patterns and clothing samples. A designer has the option to create their own patterns and submit them to the manufacturer. Another option is to submit technical drawings to the manufacturer, and the tailors/seamstresses working in the factory will hand-make the patterns or operate

a pattern-making machine to create them. Larger factories have money to invest in high-tech machines to make patterns at a faster pace, while smaller factories hand-make them. **Pattern makers** are people who do not sew and only create and cut patterns for seamstress, tailors, and fashion designers. Patterns and **pattern grading** are very important. It's best to provide physical clothing samples. This will increase the chances of your wholesale order being accurate in measurement and fit.

Step 4: Have Multiple Clothing Samples Made

Producing two samples of each style of garment is highly recommended. This will allow you to keep one for reference and one for the manufacturer to use for producing additional samples in the same style. Manufacturers will charge for each sample, and usually samples are priced at a **retail price** and not a **wholesale price**. If you decide to produce a wholesale order with the manufacturer, the price they charged you for the sample clothes will be deducted from the total price of your **wholesale order**. One benefit of having a sample made is that it allows you to prepare for sales by **testing the market.** Coordinate a photo shoot for models to model the clothing samples, and use the fashion photos for marketing your designs on social media. This allows you to learn what consumers are most interested in, and you will know exactly which designs to produce in large volumes for your wholesale order. If you are ordering samples of 20 or more designs, it's considered a **small production** and this allows you to negotiate the production price with a clothing manufacturer in China.

Step 5: Review Clothing Samples

Once you've produced multiple samples, you will be able to review them to ensure that all **stitching** is of strong quality, the fabric is correct for your garment, and that you are satisfied with the manufacturers work. Then, test the quality by wearing and washing the samples. This will allow you to know the quality of the fabric, materials, and construction of the clothes before ordering in bulk. If changes need to be made, this is the time to do it. This is your first time performing quality control so make it count! This is a back and forth communication process as much as it is a clothing manufacturing process. It can take time to perfect the samples to get exactly what you want. If your samples don't come out exactly how you want them on the first time, a factory can either make the necessary adjustments or not. If they can't make adjustments, you will know that the factory isn't capable of producing clothes up to your standards.

Step 6: Small and Mass Production
An integral part of the clothing production process is the manufacturers' **lead-time** and **production timeframe**. A lead-time is the time prior to your production getting started. The production timeframe is the time it takes to produce all of your garments. Once the factory has completed your order and quality control check, you can have the manufacturer ship all of your merchandise to you, or to the location that will sell your clothes.

Step 7: Shipping
Your final products need to be shipped to you or your client once everything is completed. Shipping costs need to be factored in to the production budget. The more products you make, the more your shipping cost will be when shipping by airplane. Prices for shipping by airplane are determined by the weight of the parcel. If you are a registered company, you can negotiate shipping cost with shipping carriers once you sign up for a business account with their company. When shipping products that are large volumes, it's cheaper to purchase a **container** and ship by **sea freight**.

Fashion Gems
Now that you are aware of the process to start and manufacture a fashion brand, I would like to share with you an alternative route to starting a clothing brand. **Trading** and **rebranding** is very popular amongst those who desire a quicker and cheaper process when it comes to designing and selling clothes. This process involves locating a clothing factory, purchasing ready-to-wear fashions from the factory's showroom, and having the factory sew your **clothing labels** into the clothes instead of using their company clothing labels. The most important tasks for rebranding clothes is purchasing clothes from a factory with good quality products, choosing

designs that you feel would be a top seller, and negotiating a wholesale price for your order. Some clothing factories will allow you to order designs from their catalog and customize the designs by ordering the clothes in the colors of your choice. Usually prices increase when any customizations are applied. Remember: all prices can be negotiated, and the larger the quantity, the more advantage you have during the negotiating process. Keep in mind, that if your budget and order is small, the production cost will be higher therefore your retail prices should be higher since you will be offering limited items. A large retail store that has a large budget or order will receive lower production prices therefore their retail prices will be cheaper.

Fashion Gem

Please make note that if you visit a manufacturer in person, the factory manager and agents will view you as a serious client. This can increase the percentages of your clothing order passing quality control. This does not mean that you have to fly to China or to another manufacturer in another country in order to receive quality service. However, if a factory manager knows that you are willing to invest time and money to visit them, they will be more willing to go the extra mile because you will be viewed as a valuable client. I recommend visiting the manufacturer once you decided that they are the factory that will produce your wholesale order. You don't have to visit the manufacturer each time you are ready to produce with them but you should establish a strong relationship in the beginning.

China vs. Korea:

Korea is 2%-3% more expensive than China when it comes to manufacturing cost but Korea has strong advantages such as:

1. It's closer to America than China therefore you save time and cost on shipping.
2. The Korea Trade Free Agreement (Korus FTA) has a trade agreement with USA which allows Americans to pay zero taxes while China's taxes are eating away at company profits because the taxes cause the overhead cost to increase.

It's up to you to research and have clothing samples made to determine which country has the best quality and price.

The illustration above was created using a fashion design software by a professional illustrator in India. Remember, when using software, you are still required to draw the designs first.

Now that you are aware of the process of manufacturing a fashion brand, it's time to learn how to produce a fashion brand in an ethical way.

5

JOIN THE TEAM AND GO GREEN

When we think of who the biggest polluters are, we might think of oil companies and smog from coal mines. But the fact is, the fashion industry is one of the most polluting industries in the world. Only a small percentage of the world's croplands are used for cotton for our clothes, yet cotton farming is responsible for a large percentage of pesticide use. Not only is that harmful to our planet, but it also harms thousands of farmers and producers each year who work in the areas with these chemicals and wastes. Due to pollution, brands are becoming increasingly mindful of how their clothes are produced. Some brands are lowering their percentage of dyes and using natural materials, while others are growing organic, pesticide-free cotton.

Eco friendly clothing is formed from natural materials that cause no level of toxicity to humans. All-natural clothes are 100 percent created out of natural material and free from all hurtful chemicals that would harm your health. Eco-friendly is a fast-developing industry allowing fashion lovers to manifest their fashion visions while keeping the environment safe at the same time. Many people are becoming aware of the chemicals used in the materials to produce clothes, as well as and the skin ailments that they cause. The advantages of using non-eco friendly materials are that they are sturdy because of the chemicals and the cost is much less.

Harvesting organic cotton is more labor-intensive because it's done without the use of chemicals.

Organic and Eco-Friendly Fabrics

Certified organic textiles are grown in controlled settings free of herbicides, pesticides, or artificial fertilizers, and are certified by different global organizations. Using organic materials benefits Mother Nature by lowering the percentage of water and energy pollution, and by making less waste throughout production. To fulfill your fashion dreams without sacrificing our health and planet, consider creating an eco-friendly clothing brand.

Organic Manufacturing

This is the method of manufacturing clothes in an organic way by using organic materials, which are grown without the inclusion of pesticides and chemicals. The fabrics that are preferred to use for manufacturing organic apparel must be in the list of organic raw materials in the manufacturing sector such as organic cotton, bamboo, hemp or soy. Ethical issues such as child labor and fair pay also play a major role in organic manufacturing. Organic clothing manufacturers usually consider the following: the condition of the land for growing organic fiber and cotton, and management of cross-pollination and weeds. The steps required to start an eco-friendly clothing brand are similar to the steps required to start a clothing brand that isn't eco friendly, except the process for an eco-friendly brand does not harm nature, animals, or people. It involves behaving with integrity, making conscious decisions, and understanding that we are all one and one with nature.

Recycle/Reuse Garments

Lets imagine that you've cleaned out your closet and ended up with a big bag of clothing that you don't like, can't fit in, or simply no longer need. But before you toss it, **tweak** it. Many fashion designers have become successful with redesigning clothes and selling them online or in a brick and mortar store. Some designers sell their pieces to **consignment stores**. The beauty of the recycle/reuse movement is that you are recycling material and creating trendy designs in fabrics that may no longer be available in stores due to the year the original garment was manufactured. A redesigned garment allows consumers to purchase garments that can't be found in any other store, and there is usually only one available for sale since it's a **reconstructed** garment. Designers have become very successful at selling reconstructed garments because the garment is considered a custom-made piece. Therefore, the garment can be sold at a higher price than a collection of mass-produced clothes that are sold in **chain stores.** Reconstructed garments are also referred to as **upcycling**. New and used garments can be redesigned and sold to consumers.

Fashion Gem

Another advantage of redesigning garments is that once you make any changes to the original garment such as removing sleeves, changing buttons, or any other changes, the design no longer belongs to the original designer. This allows you the freedom to add your clothing label to the garment.

Landfills aren't just bad for the environment; they are also bad for municipal budgets. Every year, millions of clothes end up in landfills, where they take up a massive amount of expensive space. Landfills cost millions of dollars to build and millions more every year to operate. Recycling keeps landfill costs down for cities, thereby increasing their available budget for other municipal needs.

Fashion Gem

People will give their business to companies that practice **ethical policies** and serve a higher purpose by helping the environment and communities, before they will give their business to a company that offers the same product and a lower price point. It's a win/win to go green.

Below is a fashion drawing from a beginner level fashion design student living in Shanghai, China. The drawing shows how a long, ankle length dress can be redesigned to create a short, summer dress. The designer added a belt and blazer to the dress to create a professional, chic, summer look.

6

THE FUNDAMENTALS OF BUSINESS

Introducing a clothing brand can be done in many ways. Most fashion designers will have a **launch party,** which is an invite-only party for the guest to view their new clothing brand, or they will have a fashion show to display the brand on a larger scale. Usually at launch parties and fashion shows, there are **fashion bloggers**, **fashion buyers**, **consumers**, as well as other **elite guests.** Some fashion designers will open a **brick and mortar** store while others start off with an **e-commerce store** to sell their fashion brand. Fashion designers that plan to open a brick and mortar store will usually have a **grand opening**. Fashion **retail stores** of all kinds will usually start their **branding, sales and promotions** a month or more before the store opens.

Product Branding

A clothing brand starts with a unique name, creative **logo**, and catchy **slogan**. **Trademarks** help identify the clothing brand's product and distinguish them from their **competitors**. The brand may also trademark other distinguishing features that help identify its product in the **marketplace**. For example, Louboutin's red shoe soles qualify as trademark features. A clothing brand may also **copyright** clothing designs, patterns, artwork and other creative work. A brand depends on trademarks and copyrights to protect its clothing line from cheap **knockoffs.** Be mindful of this when manufacturing your brand in another country. Every country has it's own laws therefore you should look further into how-to protect your designs while producing with a manufacturer outside of your home country.

Sales and Promotions

Whether your store specializes in one style of clothing for a small target audience, or offers a little bit of something for every shopper, fighting for consumers' dollars is a battle. Make your store stand out by promoting **specialty clothes events**, and highlight why your store is the place to shop. Sales and promotions are successful when you create a strategic **marketing plan**.

Fashion Gem
Marketing Plan Ideas:

Without a marketing strategy, your fashion brand might as well not exist. A marketing strategy is a section of your business plan that outlines the overall game plan on how you will attract customers. In some cases, a marketing strategy is confused with a marketing plan but they are different. A marketing strategy focus on what you want to achieve for your business and marketing efforts. A marketing plan will describe how you will achieve those goals.

Fashion Show: Get your fashion brand to the masses by organizing a fashion show. Try adding technology to your fashion show in order for fans to stream the live show if they aren't able to physically be there.

Hire a professional stylist during specific hours in your store. While you might want to charge customers for the stylist's services, consider offering free appointments with the payoff that customers will spend more time in-store while getting their make-over for free. If you are starting an e-commerce store, you can offer an online personal stylist. An online stylist will usually request for their client to complete a **style analysis form** to learn all about their clients fashion needs, concerns, and body measurements. This process may also require a client to submit a full body picture of themselves in order for an online stylist to know what colors and style of clothes that will compliment the clients body. Once an online stylist is aware of their clients needs, budget, and body type, they will start the process of choosing clothes from their store inventory that will deliver the look the client is going for.

Fashion party: Offer customers a promotional event, which is an invitation-only gathering. Bring out the newest clothes and mark the price tag with a reduced price. Customers will most likely purchase more than one item since they are receiving a new garment at a reduced price. This also allows the customer to purchase limited items before they are sold in the store. Try offering wine and playing upbeat music to create a fun experience to encourage customers to make a purchase. There are no limits when coordinating a fashion party and you can also make it a public event depending on your marketing strategy for this event.

Celebrity Style. Celebrities are trend-setters, but their clothing can be too expensive or hard to find. Devote a section of your store and make it a celebrity theme where shoppers can dress like their favorite celebrities at an affordable price.

If you are an independent fashion designer, I highly recommend that you register for a marketing and sales workshop or class, or purchase a reputable marketing and sales book to learn more. If you are a business with a large marketing budget, you can hire professionals to market and promote your fashion brand.

Structuring a Retail Store

Determining the company structure for a retail store is a very important part of a **business plan**. Creating a clear, detailed **operational structure** will help you decide individual responsibilities and a **chain of command**. Depending on the type of store you open, will determine your list of jobs and duties. For example: If you are a brick and mortar store, you will need a store manager, a few cashiers, and salesmen and women. Once you have created job positions and duties, you will need to plan the operational structure such as stores hours, days, employee work schedules, dates for you to purchase new **inventory**, etc. Your company budget is also important when deciding the type of company to structure.

First, decide if you are an e-commerce store or brick and mortar store. Create **departments** that you will need for your business and hire staff for each department. Below is an example of how you can structure a company.

Structuring A Company

Sales Department	Design Team	Management Team	Shipping and Handling
Sales Man/ Woman. Cashier	Fashion designers and illustrators	Store managers. The boss.	Shipping agent
Sell clothes to customers in store. Create selling plans to sell clothes.	Create new clothing designs.	Hire staff, manage the operations of the entire store. Open and close the store.	Package and ship clothing orders to online shoppers.
Working Hours: 10-18:00	Working Hours: 10-13:00	Working Hours: 10-18:00	Working hours: 10-17:00

E-Commerce Store

With advancements in technology and with the popularity of the internet, more and more people are turning to the web for a variety of purposes. An e-commerce website is a website that allows your business to sell products and services to an online audience. An increasing number of consumers are making purchases online out of convenience.

Benefits of having an online store:

1. Wider customer reach. Having an online store is a global service that allows you to sell to a larger audience in several countries.
2. Ability to open 24/7. Your customers can purchase any time of the day, which increases sales.

3. Easier set-up. An e-commerce store is usually easier to run than a brick and mortar store, and is less expensive since you will only need storage space for your inventory.
4. Reduce risk: You have a smaller staff or none, which means you have lower **overhead** cost.

Brick and Mortar Store

Nothing beats holding a product in your hand, feeling the fabric, and seeing the details-something that can't be done while shopping online. A high number of consumers want to try on the merchandise before they purchase. They want to interact with a variety of clothes before making buying decisions.

Benefits of having a brick and mortar store:

1. Customers can touch and try on clothes before purchasing.
2. Customers can receive their clothes the same day.
3. The staff can build relationships with customers during store events, which increases sales. The customers will also feel appreciated.
4. Lower shipping cost. Customers can return items to the store instead of the customer or store paying for exchanges or return shipping.
5. The store has a storage room so you don't need a warehouse like an e-commerce store. Once your company grows, you may need to add a warehouse.

Consignment Shop

Fashion designers also have the option to sell their products in a consignment shop. A consignment shop is a retail store that sells **second-hand** items or **custom-made** items from designers. Consignment shops offer designers a space to display and sell their merchandise. The shop owner will decide what they are willing to sell and for what price. The designer usually informs the store owner of the amount they would like to earn from the sale and then the store owner will add a markup to that amount so that the store can make a profit. After the sale has been completed, the owner and designer split the profits. If the products don't sell after a certain time period, the designer has the ability to retrieve the items from the consignment shop without losing any money. Each store has different requirements for consignment.

B2B

B2B or business to business, is selling your fashion brand to small or large businesses. This is also an option if you don't want to operate an e-commerce or brick and mortar store. Although you are relieved from the hassles of managing a store and possibly **wearing multiple hats,** there is a lot of risk and responsibility when selling a fashion brand to a store at wholesale prices. Large retailers usually have strict selling contracts, which will require you to have a safety budget in case your product doesn't sell in their store by the date you agreed to. When selling your fashion brand to small retailers like boutiques, the risks are lower considering that you are selling a smaller quantity of clothes. Additionally, a boutique will usually purchase your fashion brand wholesale and with no strings attached. If the brand successfully sells in their store, they will order more. If the brand is difficult to sell, most likely you will lose a buyer unless they are confident that your new designs will perform better.

Fashion Gem

I highly recommend that you complete a business plan before opening an e-commerce or brick-and-mortar store to sell your fashion brand. A business plan is the blueprint for any business owner to follow who hopes to create and operate a successful business, and it is beneficial in many ways. If you aren't confident in writing a business plan by yourself, you have the option to hire a professional to write it, or you can ask a business advisor to assist you with completing one. Business plan writing workshops are also offered to business owners during selective times throughout the year by small business development centers, and courses from business specialists can be found online. Your business plan should be completed before you start producing garments on a small or large scale with manufacturers. If you are starting a large retail store, I recommend that you hire a manager for each department.

Benefits of a business plan:

1. **Entrepreneurs**: for you to follow as a guide while you aim to successfully sell your products and grow your business. A fashion designer without a business plan to follow is like a ship sailing without a final destination. A business plan will assist you with setting company goals, learning your market, and much more.

2. **Business Partners:** to help keep you and your business partners on the same page as you execute the plans documented to successfully sell your products and grow your business. Usually business partners will work on a business plan together to avoid conflict later in regards to business decisions. You and your partner will have to agree on plans and tactics as you work on your business plan. With this method, everyone will know what is expected of them in the business.

3. **Investors:** to present to investors with the goal of securing funding to start and operate your business. Investors are most interested in the start-up expenses, capitalization, and financial plan found within the full business plan. Pitching an idea to an investor is the first step; once they are interested, the next step is submitting your business plan.

While writing your business plan, you will have to specify the type of store that you will open, along with the specifics of how the plan will operate for 1-3 years. Once you have your plan completed and the operation of your company sorted out, it's time to put the plan into action and start selling your fashion brand.

Following a business plan requires discipline, and there will be some unexpected emergencies and expenses along the way which will require you to amend the plan. Stay calm and don't panic, for this is normal. But be sure to consult with your business partners, investors, and board members throughout the amending process. If you are operating a company alone, be sure to review your successes and failures so that you can learn what's working and what's not before making any changes. For example, if you have collection of business suits for men and they haven't been sell-ing, before you invest more money to purchase a new inventory or mark down your suit collection for a clearance, try switching up your marketing material. Coordinate a lifestyle photo shoot with a model that will deliver a professional look, book a photographer that has experience in fashion photography, and choose a nice area with plenty of business buildings to create the lifestyle of a business person. Once you have quality marketing material, advertise your fashion brand through different marketing chan-nels. Your failure to sell may only require a simple solution such as creating better marketing material to hook your potential customers.

7

FASHION MARKETING

The field of **fashion marketing** covers a wide variety of positions within the business side of fashion. You could work as a fashion buyer, **customer service representative**, **retail store owner**, **retail manager**, **operations manager**, **advertiser**, and much more.

A **fashion marketer's** job is to promote fashion. Fashion marketing involves advertising, but it's more than that. Fashion marketers endorse the right fashion product at the right time to help companies reach their sales goal. Their goal is to connect the public with new fashion products, and they help set trends. This position identifies consumer lifestyle needs, develops fashion-related products and prices, and distributes and promotes them effectively to consumers. Poor fashion marketing can result in you having awesome products in your inventory that don't sell because of lack of awareness from your consumers.

Marketing is an important strategy to ensure the growth of your business. While your current customers should always be your main priority, marketing efforts can help you expand your customer base, which will result in higher sales volumes. Focus on your **signature pieces** and concentrate on the unique, **trademark** features of your signature piece that people can relate to. For example: In the 1920's Coco Chanel and Jean Patou created the infamous little black dress that was affordable yet elegant and suitable for every occasion.

One of the best methods to promote a fashion line is to send some of your products to fashion bloggers, **vbloggers** on YouTube, and influencers on Instagram. Running your marketing campaign through these platforms will make your campaign more recognized. The larger the following the blogger has, the higher the chances you have of selling your products in large volumes. Fashion marketers understand the value of influential bloggers and how they can influence an enormous amount of people without spending thousands of dollars on advertising campaigns. This type of collaboration is beneficial for an entrepreneur or company, so make sure to reach out to social media influencers as a part of your fashion marketing campaign.

Your company website will also play an important role in promoting your products to boost sales. Your website should be interactive and easy to navigate to ensure that your customers enjoy browsing and shopping from your site. Creating an app for your store is also another strategy for reaching your target audience and selling your products. There are a variety of methods in which you can promote your fashion brand, but no matter what you choose, you should always aim to be innovative.

Fashion Gem

When preparing your fashion **marketing campaign**, make sure that your signature piece is the center of attention. Some fashion marketers dedicate the whole campaign to a single piece, putting emphasis on how it will suit every person in their target audience. This marketing strategy increases your revenue because you are supplying to the masses. I highly recommend that you consult with a marketing agent, take a workshop, or read a book on marketing to learn more ways to successfully market your clothing brand.

8

FASHION SHOW AND EVENT PRODUCTION

Fashion shows debut every year for all seasons, but mostly during the Spring/Summer and Fall/Winter seasons. Usually, **fashion trends** are started during fashion shows, and they set the tone for the upcoming fashion season.

During a typical fashion show, you will witness several tasks being performed by experts in a variety of fields within the industry. For example: **Models** strut the catwalk dressed in the clothing created by fashion designers, fashion bloggers sit center row to catch a good look at the newest trends, and fashion buyers look eagerly for designs on the catwalk that have potential to be top sellers in retail stores.

The early stages of fashion show production are always exciting for an **event coordinator.** During this stage, they meet with clients, discuss their desires, and share ideas to get the ball rolling. Before the event, they'll have to convince the client that they are the right event coordinator or event company for the job. The first step is creating ideas that will best compliment the designer's vision and make their collection stand out to create a buzz. Choosing a **PR** firm to build a buzz from the media about the show is also the duty of an event coordinator. An event coordinator basically oversees the entire operation of a fashion show from start to finish.

Fashion Gem

In the mid-nineties Victoria's Secret created a buzz by introducing a lingerie line called Angel, and then decided to have annual fashion shows presenting their lingerie collection on models that wear angel wings. Since then, they have become the most-watched fashion event, with millions of viewers each year.

Event coordinators are also responsible for coordinating staff for lights and audio, ordering a runway stage, hiring **photographers**, **videographers,** and many other staff members. Having professional lighting, video, and audio can be the difference between your fashion show being the event of the season or a complete disaster. Photographing models on the runway is entirely different from photographing models in a studio. The models glide and sway, therefore it's very important that you hire photographers with experience in fashion show photography.

The backstage is where a lot of interesting things happen. It is where all of the models, designers, hairstylists, and makeup artists get everything ready for the show. Having a team of experienced videographers is important when trying to capture the creative process of the show.

Fashion designers are required to apply for fashion shows unless they are coordinating their own event. Most fashion shows require a fashion designer to pay an entry fee to showcase their collection. Fashion shows that showcase well-known clothing brands requires the fashion designer to pay a large entry fee, while fashion shows that showcase beginner clothing brands require a cheaper entry fee.

It's common for fashion designers to hire their own models, **hair stylists**, and **makeup artists,** but when a fashion designer enters a well-known fashion show, models, hair stylists, and makeup artists are included as a package deal for the entry fee that they are required to pay. Every fashion designer has their own style and theme; therefore, choosing hair stylists, models, and makeup artists to help bring their vision to life is very important.

Fashion Gem

If your target audience is professional men 30 and older, your runway models should consist of men that deliver that look. If your clothing brand is women's active wear, your runway models should be physically fit, and their hair and makeup should be simple to deliver the look of a woman who is about to work out.

Create an Engaging Atmosphere

Imagine that you enter a room full of people and see aerial ribbon dancers suspended from the ceiling, flashing lights, and hear loud music. You may think that you just walked into a circus, but you've just entered a fashion show. If you're blown away, then the event planner has done his or her job.

Having a great setup is the key to creating an atmosphere that grabs people's attention and keeps them wanting more. Choose a location that's impressive and works with the theme of the show. Use lights for striking effect at the beginning and end of the event in order to create an exciting entrance and exit. During the show, make sure the lighting is bright enough to showcase the designs and assist the photographers with capturing the event. This is very important since the show is all about the fashion. Therefore, there shouldn't be any distractions during the show.

Enhance Your Show With Technology

Fashion and tech are two industries that have danced around each other for years, but the time has finally arrived for the two to unite. Technology can be used to enhance the show for the viewers, even if they're sitting right next to the catwalk. Big screens on both sides of the runway can give the audience an up-close and personal view of the clothing worn by the models. Consider webcasting the event online along with social media hash tags to engage your virtual guests and keep them talking about all the exciting features of the show. Advertising is key for these kinds of events so utilize all your options, including social media.

Welcome to The Exciting World of *Virtual Reality*

Virtual reality is an artificial environment that is created with software and presented to the user in such a way that the user suspends disbelief and accepts it as a real environment. On a computer, virtual reality is primarily experienced through two of the five senses: sight and sound. Adding virtual reality to a fashion show makes it more exciting for guest. Because fashion is a highly visual industry, providing virtual reality for a fashion show can help grab a viewer's attention and keep it throughout the show. The reality is, virtual reality is no longer a part of some distant future and provides more than just entertainment through games. Virtual reality can revolutionize the way we present fashion.

Below is a fashion illustration of two models waiting to model an inspirational t-shirt brand for a Fall/Winter and Spring/Summer collection. The two ladies are using virtual reality to view the fashion show. The illustration was created using a design software by an experienced fashion illustrator living in India.

9

PRESENTING YOUR FASHION BRAND

It's finally here: the **launch** of your new fashion brand! The time has arrived for you to share your creations with the world. One of the first steps to take is to create a press release for your fashion brand. Now that you've spent countless hours creating your fashion brand, you can't wait around for consumers to notice it.

A professional **press release** is one of the best approaches to take to ensure that your launch is introduced to fashion bloggers, fashion buyers, and consumers. You have the option to hire a professional to write your press release, but learning to write your own press release is worthwhile and will save you money if you are an independent designer. Usually, a press release will be sent out before a fashion show, and if you hire a PR agent, this is a service that can be provided by them.

Three Tips To Write A Press Release

1. **Provide detailed information.** Tell your readers what's innovative about your fashion brand and why they should give it their attention. Provide information about the inspiration for the collection and when, where, and who founded the fashion brand. The

information in the press release also makes it easy for journalists and fashion bloggers to share vital information about your fashion brand with their **fan base** and the public. You should include information on the brand, its products, the season of the collection, and when and where the launch will take place. Adding images in the press release can help capture the attention of your readers and keep it from start to finish.

2. **Add Background Information to Your Press Release.** The background information at the end of the press release should include a brief summary of your brand, and your contact information. This will make it easy for fashion bloggers, PR teams, and other interested parties to communicate with you about your launch.

3. **Make Your Press Release Visual.** It's no secret that visuals excite readers and press release perform best when using visuals to market a product. Include the best image at the top of your press release and create a layout for the press release that makes it easy for readers to find the exact information that they are looking for. Not only will this make your press release more exciting, but it will also set the bar for your new fashion brand.

Fashion Gem

If you are an **entrepreneur** starting a fashion brand on a small scale, distribute your press release through all free **media outlets**. If you have a budget to play with, hire a professional PR company to effectively get your press release to the public. You can also hire a **college intern** majoring in marketing to write the press release in order to relieve yourself of extra work while at the same time keeping your expenses low by not hiring a PR company. You can have the best fashion brand in the world but if no one knows about you, your brand might as well not exist. Learn more about how to write a press release by doing your research.

10

CRITICAL THINKING QUESTIONS AND ACTIVITIES

1. You are in a foreign country on a business trip to source textiles. While walking down the street in a busy outdoor market, you decide to walk down a less crowded street to get to your destination. Out of nowhere, three unarmed men try to rob you. How do you plan to handle this situation?

2. You are in a foreign country and can't speak the native language. You need to give the tailors instructions to make your samples but you didn't make arrangements for a translator to visit the factory with you. You have a language translator app but it's not translating your messages to the tailors like you expected. It's important that you submit the order today. How are you going to handle this situation?

3. You received your wholesale order and you discovered defects with several garments during your quality control check. You are located in America and the factory is located in China. After informing the factory of the problem, the manager of the factory offers you a credit to your next order. A percentage of your inventory isn't sellable and you need the garments now. This situation changes the numbers for your sales goals and expected income because the

garments can't be repaired and sold. Your next order from China is scheduled to arrive to you in 60 days. What are you going to do to meet you sales goals this month?

4. You paid to have a tailor/factory to produce your fashion brand. When picking up your samples you noticed that one of your designs was copied and is being sold to another company by the manufacturer. How are you going to address this issue?

5. You have a new client/buyer with a large spending budget. You ensured the client/buyer that they would receive their order of custom made garments within four weeks. You immediately start the process of the order by choosing and ordering fabrics online. The fabric store informs you that you will receive your order of fabric in three days. You received your order in three days but 1 out of 6 fabrics wasn't the fabric that you ordered. Your client specifically asked for certain colors therefore you have to send the fabric back to the fabric store in order for them to exchange the fabric. Because you have to mail the fabric back, it will take 3 days for the fabric store to receive the fabric. The fabric store informs you that their warehouse has to send the fabric to you and it will take 3-5 days because they are located in another city. The correct fabric finally arrives at the tailor shop but they inform you that it's a busy time of the year therefore producing your order will take four weeks instead of two weeks as promised. This does not include the time-frame for the clothing order to be mailed to you. You also have to mail the order to your client and that will take between 3-5 business days. Now that you are aware that your order won't be delivered by the time promised to your client/buyer, how do you plan to handle this situation to ensure that you wont loose a valuable client/buyer?

6. You are working a full time job and running your online start up company at the same time. At the moment, you are using your home to store your inventory but there isn't anyone there during the day to sign and receive your packages from manufacturers. You also need to mail packages to your online shoppers before the post

office close. You are released from your full time job after the business hours of the post office. This issue is causing you to mail your orders late. How do you plan to solve this problem?

7. You submitted a wholesale clothing order to a clothing manufacturer and they informed you that your clothing order can be shipped directly to your client/buyer from their manufacturer. You agree to the arrangements but then you receive a call from the manufacturer informing you that your shipping container got held up at customs due to mistakes on the shipping forms. For each day that the port has to hold your shipping container, you will be charged holding fees. This is called **demurrage**, "cargo that stays at a terminal too long." Whether the port charges $85 or $300 per container, just a few days of late charges for 5 containers could cost you thousands of dollars. If for some reason your cargo gets held up at the terminal for more than a week, chances are the daily fees will increase. You didn't create an emergency budget for this order and now it's a strong chance that the order will arrive late to your client/buyer. Keep in mind that the client/buyer has sales goals to meet for their retail company therefore receiving their inventory as scheduled is very is important. If this client/buyer continues to order wholesale clothes from you, this will be a contract that can change your life by helping your business prosper financially. How are you going to solve this problem? You don't have the funds to pay the shipping delay charges to customs and your client needs their order by a certain date.

8. You offer exclusive personal styling services to clients that have big spending budgets. You shipped the clothing orders to your clients and all of the garments were too big. You market your personal styling services as made-to-measure, which involves the client submitting their body measurements to you and your tailors are expected to make those garments according to the measurements. Since this is an exclusive personal styling service and the garments are made-to-measure, your clients are expecting their garments to be the perfect fit because they are spending thousands of dollars

per order. A few clients have been informing you that they aren't completely satisfied with their garments because they end up having to pay expensive fees to a local tailor to alter the garments. What's your plan to gain your clients trust back and keep them shopping with you? How will you improve measurement and fit moving forward?

9. You are a fashion designer working for an internationally known fashion firm. You purchase fabric for new designs but you didn't take into consideration that the fabric you were purchasing was too thick and stiff for the style you were aiming for therefore the finished garments didn't look the same as the free, flowing garments on your sketch. You spent 90% of your budget on this order of samples that doesn't meet the company's expectations. You have two more weeks before you meet the deadline for this order. How do you plan to move forward and present clothing samples to your company?

10. Madison's children's clothing brand is currently being manufactured and assembled in China but the finishing's are done in America. Which of the following can Madison add to the clothing labels?
    a) Made in America
    b) Made in China
    c) Both

Practice

You were given $60,000 to open a boutique. Create a financial forecast to determine how you would allocate your budgets for a future period. Example: $10,000 inventory budget, $25 marketing budget, etc. Discuss your financial forecast with your classmates.

With a partner, role-play an American fashion buyer of a boutique and a Chinese wholesaler who are negotiating wholesale prices for women's handbags. The retail price for the handbag you want is selling for $150 per bag. The wholesaler in China is aware of this retail price and he/she plans to earn a nice profit from this sale. Buyer, before you start negotiating, ask yourself the following questions:

a) How many handbags are you going to purchase?
b) How much do you want to pay for each handbag?
c) What's your ideal profit margin for the handbags?

Discuss your outcome with the class.

With a partner, role-play a journalist for a famous fashion magazine interviewing a famous fashion designer during fashion week in NYC. Be prepared to act out the conversation for your classmates and the class will provide feedback.

With a small group, answer and discuss these questions based on your knowledge.

a) What's an RN number?
b) What's a customs broker?
c) What is an IPR and why is it important?
d) What is tariff cost? Why is this important to know when importing/exporting?
e) Which type of clothing is the highest seller? Activewear, swimwear, or business attire?

With a partner, create marketing material for current fashion trends. Schedule and coordinate a mini fashion photo shoot. Creatively present your marketing material to the class.

With a partner, complete a specs sheet for a t-shirt brand. Give the manufacturer information for three different sizes. Share your specs sheet with another group and provide feedback.

The showroom you work at just accepted a new Fall/Winter collection of men and women business attire. Work with your partners and create innovative marketing material to promote this clothing brand. Example: a flyer, poster, newspaper ad, commercial, etc. Present your marketing material to the class and the class will provide feedback. Use the fashion illustration below.

GLOSSARY

Discovering Your Passion:

Designing: the process of producing a drawing to show the look of a fashion design.

Sketches: rough or unfinished drawings often made to assist in making a completed fashion design.

Inspirations: an unconscious burst of creativity to do or design something

Color combinations: combinations of individual colors.

Photo props: accessories, furniture, or products used to create a theme for a photo.

Fashion Tips: ideas for how to wear fashion products.

Fashion blogger: a person that shares helpful tips on many things such as clothing, accessories, beauty tips, and trends in various apparel markets.

Theme: an idea that recurs in a work of art.

Introduction to Fashion Design:

Consumer: a person who purchases goods and services for personal use.

Target audience: a particular group of consumers that you intend to advertise your clothes to. Example: children, age 5-10.

Fashion Seasons: fashion divides itself into seasons in order for you to dress for the weather. Spring/Summer is from January-June. Fall/Winter is from July-December.

Leather: a material made from the skin of an animal by tanning or a similar process.

Wool: the fine, soft, curly or wavy hair forming the coat of a sheep, goat, or similar animal.

Suede: leather with the flesh side rubbed to make a velvety nap.

Velvet: a closely woven fabric of silk, cotton, or nylon, that has a thick, short pile on one side.

Lace: a fine open fabric, typically one of cotton or silk, made by looping, twisting, or knitting thread in patterns; used especially for trimming garments.

Sheer: very thin fabric.

Twill: weave (fabric) so that it has a surface of diagonal parallel edges.

Heavy Cottons: a thicker layer of cotton.

Collections: an assembly of fashion designs to create a theme.

Silk: thread or fabric made from the fiber produced by the silkworm.

Chiffon: a light, sheer fabric typically made of silk or nylon. Mostly used to produce garments that require stiff fabric to hold a shape within the design.

Cotton: a soft, white, fibrous substance that surrounds the seeds of a tropical and subtropical plant and is used as textile fiber and thread for sewing clothes.

Taffeta: a fine, lustrous silk or similar synthetic fabric with a crisp texture.

Woven: a cloth formed by threading fabric through a process of interlacing.

Fashion Forward: a person or a style of clothing that is very fashionable.

Formal Attire: Clothing suitable for a wedding, formal dinner, or dance. Usually a dark-colored suit and tie, white dress shirt, or a long evening dress.

Attire: clothes, especially formal ones.

Polyester: a fabric made from polyester fiber.

Print Fabric: fabric with designs painted or printed on it.

Blue Jean: also known as denim. A sturdy cotton twill fabric, typically blue; used mostly for blue jeans and overalls.

Ready-to-wear: clothes made for the masses and sold through stores; off-the-rack rather than made to order for an individual customer.

Fabric Story: a particular fabric or color that is consistently used throughout the collection for each fashion design.

Specs: a detailed working description of each fashion design. This includes seam measurements, the type of fabric to be used, and instructions for placement of buttons, zippers, or embellishments.

Manufacture: to make something" or "the making of".

Merchandising: branded products used to promote a particular fashion collection.

Retailers: companies that sell clothes to the public in relatively small quantities.

Fashion Illustrator: a person who draws or creates digital fashion designs for magazines, books, or advertising.

Fashion Illustration: is the art of communicating fashion ideas in a visual form that originates with illustration, drawing and painting and also known as fashion sketching.

Fashion Croquis: a rough draft or a sketch of a female or male body mainly used to help a fashion designer create a fashion design on a model.

Creating A Fashion Portfolio

Fashion Portfolio: a set of pieces of creative work collected by someone to display their skills.

Sketches: a rough or unfinished drawing or painting.

Technical Flats/Technical Drawings: a detailed drawing with seam measurements and the details of material needed to make your clothes.

Theme: an idea that reoccurs in art and fashion. Example: the color red is used for all of your designs. Example: Flower print is used for every design.

Seam Measurements: Measurements for each seam of a garment. Examples: the zipper is 5 inches long; the buttonholes are 2 inches long.

Body Measurements: The measurements of a human body. Example: chest, arms, waist, hips, legs, crotch, height.

Body Shape: the shape of a human body. Example: a wide chest and small legs.

Apparel: clothes.

Vision Board: a collage of images, pictures, and affirmations of your dreams, goals, and things that make you happy.

Mood Board: an arrangement of images, materials, pieces of text, etc., intended to project a particular style or concept.

Fashion Illustration: refer to *Intro to Fashion Design* vocabulary words.

Shading: the darkening or coloring of an illustration.

Seamstress: a woman who earns her living by sewing. Seamster is a male.

Tailor: a person whose occupation is making fitted clothes such as suits, pants, and jackets to fit individual customers.

Embellishments: a decorative detail or feature added to clothes to make it more attractive.

Garment: an item of clothing; another word used for clothes.

Fashion Collage: a way to put your fashion ideas on paper or digitally.

Process: a series of actions or steps taken in order to achieve a particular end.

Series: a set of books, maps, or other documents created in a common format or under a common title.

Specs: Spec sheets help to produce accurate samples, which improves the turnaround time and simplifies communication during all stages of manufacturing and quality control. Spec sheets include detailed technical drawings, construction notes, finished garment measurements, fabric, material, and trim details

Also known as specification sheet.

Manufacturing A Clothing Brand:

Clothing Sample: a garment used to determine the final fabric and measurements for your small order; Quality samples are used to present to fashion buyers and consumers to test the market.

Style: a particular design of clothing. Example: shorts, pants, blouse.

Sewing Techniques: the skills or ability to sew clothes.

Quality: the standard of the clothes measured against other popular clothing brands; Good quality or bad quality.

Quality Control: a process to test all of the clothes after production to meet company standards.

Pattern: a template used as a guide to sew clothes.

MOQ: minimum order quantity; this number is determined by the factory.

Clothing Production: the action of making or manufacturing the clothes from raw material.

Raw Material: materials such as fabric, buttons, and zippers.

Import Charges: the charges incurred when bringing products into the country from abroad for a sale.

Export: shipping products out of the country to another country.

Production Cost: the cost to sew the clothes.

Small Production: a small collection of clothes; usually 10-50 pieces of clothes. Large production is usually 60 or more.

Test the Market: marketing clothes to the public to learn which designs are popular to ensure your clothes will sell.

Stitching: a row of thread sewn onto clothes.

Lead Time: the time prior to your production getting started. The consultation and negotiation process of having your clothing collection produced.

Production Time: the time it takes to produce your clothing order.

Sea freight: shipping clothes in a container on a boat by sea.

Retail: the sale of goods to the public in relatively small quantities.

Retail Cost: the total price charged for a product sold to a customer, which includes the manufacturer's cost plus a retail markup.

Wholesale Cost: the selling of goods in large quantities to be retailed by others.

Rebranding: changing the corporate image of a company or organization.

Clothing Labels: a physical textile labeling on garments. A wash care label on garments.

Ready to Wear Clothes: is the term for factory-made clothing, sold in finished condition in standardized sizes.

Shipping Container: is a container with strength suitable to withstand international shipment, storage, and handling.

Pattern Grading: is the process of turning base size or sample size patterns into additional sizes using a size specification sheet or grading increments.

The Fundamentals of Business:

Launch Party: a celebration of a team's hard work and introduction of a new clothing brand or store.

Brick-and-mortar: a physical location for a store.

E-commerce: an online store.

In-house Brand: a clothing brand created and sold by a clothing store.

Grand Opening: the first day a store opens and accepts transactions.

Product Branding: a creative way to distinguish a fashion brand from other brands.

Sales and Promotions: strategies used to sell merchandise.

Competitors: a company that has a similar business structure as you.

Marketplace: a group of people that purchase products.

Marketing Plan: a creative plan to introduce your merchandise to the public and sell your product.

Business Plan: a plan created to show future objectives, goals, strategies, and how to achieve them.

Company Expenses: purchases made for the company to continue operating.

Logo: a symbol or design to represent a company.

Slogan: a memorable phrase used in advertisement.

Trademark: a symbol, word, or words legally registered or established to use as representing a company or product.

Copyright: the exclusive legal right given to a person to print, publish, perform, or film.

Operational Structure: defines how activities such as task allocation, coordination, and supervision are directed toward the achievement of organizational aims.

Chain of Command: an official hierarchy of authority that dictates who is in charge of whom, and of whom permission must be asked. Example: the store manager is in charge of the store employees, and a branch manager is in charge of all store managers at different locations.

Company Departments: a normal corporate structure consisting of various departments that contribute to the company's overall mission and goals. Examples: sales department, customer service department.

Retail Store: A **store** that sells smaller quantities of products or services to the general public.

Specialty Clothes Event: a special event created to promote and sell your fashion brand.

Entrepreneur: a person who organizes and operates a business or businesses.

Business Partner: a person who, along with another person, plays a significant role in owning, managing, or creating a company together.

Investor: a person that provides money to a company with the expectation of achieving a profit.

Elite Guest: a most valued guest.

Fashion Blogger: a person that may write about many things such as specific items of clothing and accessories, beauty tips, and trends in various apparel markets, and shares that writing with the public directly through their own outlet.

Fashion Buyer: a person employed to select and purchase clothes and accessories for a large retail store to stock and sell.

Knock Off: a copy that sells for less than the original; broadly: a copy or imitation of someone or something popular.

Overhead: operating costs or expenses.

Fashion Marketing:

Fashion Buying: buyers have to anticipate where styles are going and what will catch the consumers' attention. Not every new style will make it to retail stores; therefore, fashion buyers make decisions about what and how much to sell based on their knowledge of market trends.

Fashion Marketing: the process of examining fashion trends, helping retailers stock fashion brands, coordinating sales, and promoting goods.

Fashion Marketing Managers: people who oversee the branding and advertising of a company's new or existing products. They often monitor consumer reactions to marketing campaigns and products. A fashion marketing manager is usually in charge of a team of lower-level fashion marketers.

Customer Service Representative: a person whose job it is to interact with customers to handle complaints, process orders, and provide information about an organization's products and services.

Retail Manager: a person that manages a retail store and oversees the tasks of employees.

Operations Manager: a person whose job it is to oversee their organization's production of goods and/or services. They oversee various departments, such as purchasing, warehousing, and manufacturing.

Advertiser: a person that notifies the public of something new.

Fashion Marketers: professionals who work in fashion marketing and merchandising.

Marketing: the action or business of promoting and selling products or services, including market research and advertising.

Staple Pieces: a fashion brand's strongest design, also known as a signature piece, that is used for branding. A design that is the center of attention while promoting a clothing brand.

Fashion Show and Event Production:

Fashion Buyer: a person who purchases clothes from a fashion wholesaler or a showroom at a wholesale prices and sells the clothes in his/her clothing store.

Fashion Wholesaler: a person who sells clothes to fashion buyers at a wholesale price. A fashion buyer will usually purchase the clothes from a clothing factory at a discounted rate.

Wholesale: a discounted rate, or half-price, for clothes or goods.

Fashion Illustrator: a person who draws or paint a fashion design. They focus on delivering the visual for a fashion designer who doesn't posses drawing skills.

Fashion Designer: a person who creates designs for clothes. Some fashion designers can draw their own designs, while designers who don't draw tell their vision to a fashion illustrator who then draws or paints the fashion designs.

Fashion Blogger: A person who writes a story about fashion designers, clothing brands, fashion trends, fashion stores, and all things related to fashion, and publishes it on a website for the public to read. They also host fashion shows.

Makeup Artist: a person who applies makeup to models for fashion shows, commercials, photo shoots, and events.

Hair Stylist: a person who provides hair styling to models for fashion shows, commercials, photo shoots, and other events related to fashion.

Fashion Stylist: a person who styles the models with a fashion designer's clothing brand for fashion shows, photo shoots, commercials, and events related to fashion.

Event Coordinator: a person who plans a fashion show and hires the staff needed to operate the show. They also rent the venue for a fashion show and order everything needed such as a stage, lights, and chairs.

Fashion Photographer: a person who takes photos at a fashion show, for clothing photo shoots, and all events related to fashion. Their concentration is fashion photography.

Fashion Videographer: a person who films a fashion show, clothing commercials, and all things related to fashion. Their concentration is fashion.

PR Team/Public Relations: a person or group of people who manage and spread information about a business to the public. They create advertising ideas for clothing companies.

Presenting Your Fashion Brand:
Launch: a marketing strategy consisting of a carefully planned and scheduled sequence of events with the goal of make an impactful introduction.
Press Release: an official statement issued to the public giving information on a particular matter.
Fan Base: fans of your clothing brand.
Media Outlet: a publication or broadcast program that provides news and feature stories to the public through various distribution channels. This includes newspapers, magazines, radio, television, and the internet.
College Intern: a student who works for experience or credit, often for free; an internship consists of an exchange of services for experience between the college intern and an organization.

CHECKLIST AND MATERIALS

MATERIALS

1. **Sketch Pencils**: HB and 2B pencils, charcoal pencil for shadowing.
2. **Markers:** Chartpak A, Prismacolor.
3. **Ink Pens:** PIGMA 005, 05 for dark backgrounds.
4. **Drawing Paper:** bleed-proof paper that fits into your portfolio. Slightly see-through if you are tracing over a croquis.
5. **Ruler:** any hand-sized ruler should do.
6. **Colored Pencils**: any box of pencils that have colors for a variety of skin tones.
7. **Fashion Portfolio:** a variety of portfolios are available.
8. **Poster Board:** any 11 x 14 size poster board.
9. **Fashion Magazines:** any fashion magazine that inspires you.
10. **Glue:** preferably a glue stick.
11. **Scissors:** any pair of sharp-edged scissors.
12. **Eraser:** preferably one with a thin tip that doesn't leave residues.

CHECKLIST

Fashion Portfolio	
Clothing Manufacturer	
Business Plan/Marketing Plan	

ABOUT THE AUTHOR

Shawnie Grant started her professional career within the fashion industry in 2009 when she founded a charity organization Tailored Hearts, which reconstructs gently worn garments, and donates them to teenage girls in need living in Houston, Texas. She has years of experience in fashion design, global fabric sourcing, import/export, as well as research and development through her business Tailored Boutique, which was started in 2013. Her experience extends to the media world, where she co-hosted fashion segments to promote her clothing brand Tailored on a local new channel in Houston, KHOU 11, which is a CBS-affiliated television station. She began her personal journey with *Fashion Beyond Borders: Exploring the Global Fashion Industry* in 2015 when she made the decision to move to Shenzhen, China to work side-by-side with local clothing manufacturers to produce her clothing brand Tailored. During that time, she started writing fashion curriculums and taught them in Shenzhen, Shanghai, and Morocco. In 2017, she taught *Fashion Beyond Borders: Exploring The Global Fashion Industry* curriculum at New York University Shanghai in Shanghai, China to high school students desiring to start careers within the fashion industry. She followed with *Fashion Beyond Borders: Exploring the Global Fashion Industry* course book, which is now sold globally, offering countless others the opportunity to learn the necessary steps to start and manufacture a fashion brand. Shawnie was the first fashion consultant to teach a fashion course at New York University Shanghai NYUSPS. Shawnie is currently a graduate student in University of Houston MBA program concentrating in international business. The information in this book was developed from Shawnie's personal experiences while studying and working abroad. Learn more about Tailored Boutique's fashion consulting services at www.tailoredboutique.com.

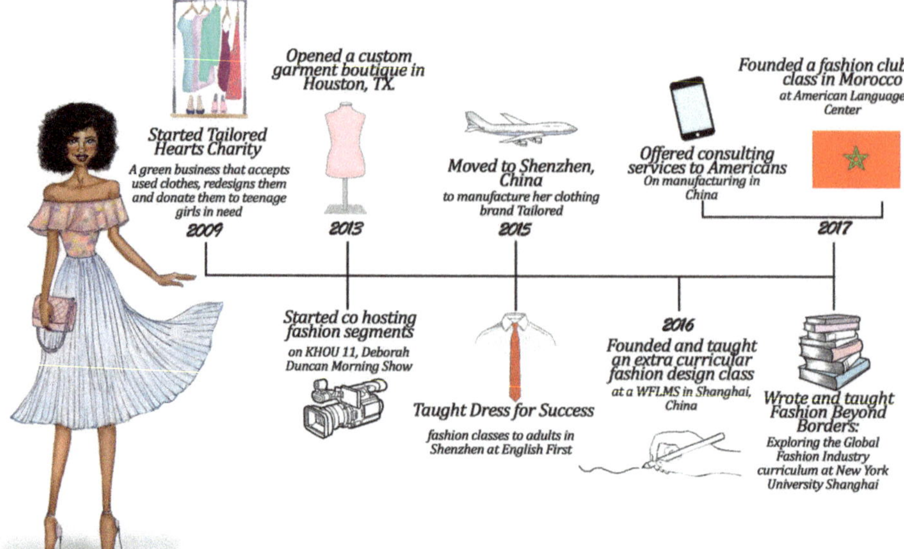
Started Tailored Hearts Charity
A green business that accepts used clothes, redesigns them and donate them to teenage girls in need
2009
Opened a custom garment boutique in Houston, TX.
2013
Started co hosting fashion segments
on KHOU 11, Deborah Duncan Morning Show
Moved to Shenzhen, China
to manufacture her clothing brand Tailored
2015
Taught Dress for Success
fashion classes to adults in Shenzhen at English First
Offered consulting services to Americans
On manufacturing in China
2017
Founded a fashion club class in Morocco
at American Language Center
2016
Founded and taught an extra curricular fashion design class
at a WFLMS in Shanghai, China
Wrote and taught Fashion Beyond Borders:
Exploring the Global Fashion Industry curriculum at New York University Shanghai

9 780692 179543